A Year in Verse

Contributors
Victoria Pearce
Mary Scarborough
Sarah Scott-Cruz
Leisl Seigler
Catherine Uritis
Benjamin Yates
Natalia Yépez-Frias
Introduction by
Maryanna Jensen

1

www.ChironPublicatons.com
innerQuest is a book imprint of Chiron
Publications

Editors: Benjamin Yates, Sarah Scott-Cruz,
        Leonard Cruz
Cover art by Catherine Uritis
Interior Design by Benjamin Yates
Cover design by Benjamin Yates and Steven Buser
Printed in the United States of America

With grateful hearts we dedicate this book to those who took part in our art: Jenny Kate Till, Jonathan Councell, and Maryanna Jensen. Thank you for your support, encouragement, and, most importantly, love.

TABLE OF CONTENTS

Preface

To the World–

Here we are. Voices. The thing is, voices
end; voices retreat and fade and run out of oxygen
or will, which ever comes first. Who are we, books
with voices, to you? Here I am, another among the
multitude. I hold a collection of voices, a chorus of
heartstrings, a communion of souls. Whispered
secrets in passageways, masks shed among
friends, ideas shouted from the treetops—lend
your ear to these moments of clarity and
confusion. World, what are you, what am I,
without these stories? This, my mere beginning,
tells stories of stories of stories, as my brothers tell;
whether in libraries on shelves or in piles under
clothes; whether crisp as a bright-eyed
entrepreneur or musty as a curded-waspy scholar.
I present you my seven voices as a celebration of
thought, an attempt of action, and ultimately a
revolution.

Despite all failure, these words I carry succeed in proclaiming the miracle of human consciousness. If there were nothing, this would still be something.

Hamlet thinks and thinks and speaks and speaks. In my case, these words are an act. No matter how imperfect, rudimentary, or subtle, there is meaning behind each poem. What is Hamlet without the finale? What is Hamlet without his act, without his death? Just as Hamlet is held above as an example, so am I an example. There is more life in the moments in which we, wide-eyed, are brave enough to embrace the ends, than in an un-momentous life in which we close our eyes, cowards in every embrace. There is more in knowing than not knowing, there is more in loving than not loving, there is more in trying than not trying. Now you see World, victory is nothing without the struggle of my voices.

Do I capture what I claim to capture? Is my limited space on the shelf, with numbered pages, with numbered voices, with numbered days, enough? Listen to skylark or nightingale, wind or season, for the tales told amongst the age-tinged pages are tales of you. You surround our voices; you are the materials for the artists, the songs for the singers, and the oyster for their work. Do not shake, for the interdependency began long before I! You turn because they know you turn, you change because they know you change; you are Nature because they have called it so.

With so many contradictions—the spiritual and the physical, the clouds and the ground, experience and innocence—the webs are tangled; does that make it one web or many, does that mean time is a circle or a line? For these reasons and in this way, when you revolve, you incite a revolution. Let my written voices reach the curious squinters so that together all these pilgrims may find eternal truth. Let us, you and I, watch: watch as they stroll and skip and sigh!

Thank you for the gift of opportunity you have given my voices! There is no greater treasure on this earth than to participate. Emily Dickinson, an echoing voice, wrote: "this is my letter to the world, that never wrote to me." Oh, but I've caught you, World! You have written all voices, otherwise how could they write? You write in tree and trial, in bird and brick, in soil and sound, in memory and man.

In the end are we not, all of us, truly, completely, irrevocably stolen from ourselves as a testimony for all mankind to that which is greater? There is an eternity that even words cannot express. I speak of all the things said and unsaid, heard and unheard, thought and un-thought, and even of all that is and is not. Taste this sweet clarity! Let me be an almsgiving to the silences of books, though our pages ring out, and to the unwritten words between the lines, though our voices write with fury to fulfill them. It is quite simple; I am a part of something, a brick on a bridge, between what lies beneath your dirt and the ever-vaster heavens above.

Sincerely,

A Year in Verse
As recorded by Natalia Yépez-Frias

Introduction

Teaching literature is a paradoxical endeavor. The task demands considerable preparation and clear goals, simultaneously requiring that such plans and goals be held with a loose hand and set aside for something greater. At its best, this venture means providing the space for students not only to discover something new about themselves and the world through their encounter with literature, but also to craft their own works in response. This year, I was fortunate enough to host a group of students who made my job delightful. They are ardent in their reading and respectful in their analysis; moreover, these students are poets in their own right. This collection is the culmination of their study of literature to date. It evinces humility through constraint to forms, courage in exposing their thoughts, and dedication to beauty. Included here are pithy, metered epigrams; the elaborate metaphors of metaphysical conceits; and those highly structured and constraining 14-liners with a glorious tradition, sonnets. Free verse, travel poems, responses to specific poets, and nonsense poems—in in which sounds and syntax carry more weight than definitions—are also present. It has been my pleasure and honor to guide these students through their study of British literature this year, and I am excited to see how they call forth truth, beauty, and goodness into this twisted yet, as Hopkins says, deep down fresh world. May their works teach and delight you, as these students have taught and delighted me this year.

Maryanna Jensen
Upper School Literature Teacher
Veritas Christian Academy
April 2015

Victoria Pearce

Tori Pearce has green eyes and loves to dance, to travel, and to be outdoors. Passionate about people and other cultures, Tori hopes to work in community development. She leaves organization in her wake. In her poetry, Tori stands steadfast, navigating storms by following and offering words of light and hope.

Life as a Spruce

My life as a growing spruce;
A small sapling, in the truth.
Winding branches stretch up to the
Sun,
Reaching toward their goal 'til time is
done.
Rays of light pierce through the leaves,
A layer of my opened heat brightly
gleams.
Stormy gales may come and go,
But there's one thing that I do know:
Whatever shakes this little tree,
She is more than what the eye can see.

A Moment of Serene Joy

Knobbly and sprawling roots
Burrowing into dark damp earth,
Veins invaded, filled throughout.
Branching limbs, lofty swaying,
Casting shady shadowstreams;
Foliage full, fanning light,
Bright heavens bordered above.
Soft clouds, sweet music medley;
Heart's earnest outpouring.
Voices in pair–as one blended–
Simple awe, and whispered wonder.

Truth spills out, snippets sung,
A portrait of perfection.
Bark's rough ridges at back,
Grass's tender rustle, livening,
Touching us as Spirit.
Silence, a sanctuary safe;
Hemmed in, haven whole.
Wall of mossy stone surrounds,
Blocks of world, light intermittent.
Wordless talking, kindred souls,
Sharing love, and sharing life.

Pancake Rocks

August 6, 2014
Punakaiki, New Zealand

I am alone, standing here atop thinly layered
seaside socks that line the shore in stacks.
The weather is chilling and blustery, coming
straight up from the sea spray just below my feet.
Rows of breakers endlessly tumble and crash
upon each other, creeping closer and closer as they
mount higher and higher.
Huge waves swell at the base of my rocks and
splash up, catching the blazing sunlight behind in
a few seconds of paradise.
Around my toes thick sea foam lingers, filling the
rock crevices and shaking like jello in the steady
wind.
A distinct smell tickles my nose, the strong salty
smell of the sea, mixed with the slightest hint of
coming rain.
And the music, oh the music of the sea – soft shhh
as water pours in sheets over sandy shore, loud
clap of thunder as wave after wave crashes into
tall rocks, sudden caww of seagulls flying
overhead.
What a beautiful scene it is, and I am but another
standing in awe of the way evening orange sun
reflects upon the crest of every tumbling wave and
turns each layer of rock a shining golden hue.

All is perfectly new.

Kaikoura Drive

August 7, 2014
Kaikoura, New Zealand

Gently sloping green hills line the base of
towering snow-capped mountains with jagged
peaks.
It is grassy and spotted with trees, scrawny
scraggly trees with leaves so paper thin you can
almost see through them in the sunlight.
Tall mountain ridges dusted with snow, hiding
their rough rock formations, bracing themselves
against strong stinging winter wind.
River of clear turquoise eddies around the valley
floor, leaving behind her mark on every smoothed
pebble and softened stone.
A line of upwards-reaching tree limbs sharply
defined by the sun's striking silhouette atop the
ridge.
Lightly frosted foliage, a dusting of snow like
powdered sugar, fades into green as altitude
decreases.
Sheep, woolly and dirtied with mud, grazing on
knobby knolls by the roadside, separated simply
by rusty barbed wire and weathered wood
stumps.
Trickling streams of cold fresh spring water leave
behind glimmering pools and puddles, natural
still mirrors reflecting blue sky above.

Deserted, not another person in sight.
Yet not abandoned nor neglected, but natural,
untouched, whole.
All is as is should be, a haven of beauty and peace.

Dunedin Cliff

Dunedin, New Zealand
August 11, 2014

Shirt plastered to sticky skin
wind whipping all around
brisk morning run along cliffs
burning legs and panting breath
chest rising up down up down
smell of salt and taste of grit
lingering sunrise in blue sky
strips of colored light above water
waves of clear turquoise below
crashing tumbling onto sandy shore
steep rock face worn away by sea
year after year of ever-rolling tide
rise and fall of green on left
hanging moss-like over cliff edge
pastures spotted with sleepy sheep
lungs filled stinging and fresh
sound of seagulls and of sea
of my own breath in out in out
steady new alive and free

Love Leaves

That time of year when yellow leaves do lie
A'scattered in the trees of harvest red;
That field where naught of young love's dreams
hath died,
Nor naught but words of deepest thanks hath
said.
That time of year when white a'covers all
In blankets of the bitt'rest chill so old,
Yet warms brown leaves with snowflakes as they
fall;
A tale of greater hope hath ne'r been told.
That time of year when spring's first sun arrives
To shower green leaf'd kisses 'pon the earth;
When young loves' dreams do burst before their
eyes,
And blissful joy at last they find unearth'd.
Oh that that time of year would steady stay!
Yet fear no more. For all time has its way.

A Heart of Shells

Broken
Shattered
Smashed
Brittle
Are the pieces of our hearts,
These shells, our inmost depth,
Our soul's identity
Our sleeve's decoration,
and yet we think we are whole.

Mending
Fixing
Forgiving
Molding
Are the things of the Lord,
God our God, the utmost king,
Our one lasting lover,
And yet we think we can heal.

Two sets of razor sharp pieces
Uniquely cracked by lines of experience
Together come in symbolic shape:
A heart, our blessed brokenness beating,
Mission of divine healing,
Portrait of human hope.

Two hearts unwhole and holey,
Yet made whole through holiness,

Completed in Christ,
Defragmented by friendship.
These pieces, now one,
Mend together by our love,
Hold fast by his endless grace,
And now we know we are whole and healed.

First Springlingly Day at the Parkarark

Smooth sunshine slitherslathered them
with sweat,
Letherlathered their limp limbs with
liltylight breeze,
Wishweshwashed underneath white
willowillowy clouds,
And dripdrapdropped like dandyflowers
from their dirty dermafingers.

Flying frisbees flingfloogflung from their
fiery fingers,
And all felt haphaphappy in that lellow
field.
There was no snippersnappering nor
gruggy grangling between these friends,
Only yupptey yippering and
gingleangling giggling.

Petals and Toes

Smooth and soft are merging petals and toes,
Petals and toes awak'ning to first light,
Yawning, squirming, writhing out of secret;
Shells of protection burst and un-enclose
The folded flower, the newborn sans sight;
A sight exciting the start of pure life.

Pure life so delicate, so free, yet bound
By stems, vines, cords, and sinews to the end -
The end, the end that will wither all skin.
The now-old newborn's dying cry will sound,
Worn flowers will crunch under life's harsh bend;
Petals and toes, mere petals and toes twinned:
Birth and growth and life and death,
Worth our rejoicings for all that has been.

The Greek Plaka

Round necks of pasty white,
Round necks of darkened black,
Round necks of tanned Greek skin
These colors wind themselves.
Apricot,
Azure,
Terracotta,
Turquoise,
Sable,
Sienna,
Silver:
These colors coil round our necks,
Tassels twisting in the wind,
Tickling our noses and rosy cheeks,
Blending color with color,
Natural with artificial, just as
Scarf to human,
Race to race,
Every face to every face.
Blue,
Brown,
Green,
Orange,
Purple,
Red,
Yellow:
These colors common to all with breath

Tie together in fabric folds these
humans,
These bustling gawking tourists,
These finagling gypsy sellers,
These everyday citizens;
All are scarves.
Blended,
Bound,
Connected,
Looped,
Layered,
Mingled together,
All the scarf of humanity,
The colors of lives,
The color of life.

Let Me Love You

"Come to me all you who are weary and
burdened, and I will give you rest."

Girl, won't you let me love you?
Turn your tear-stained face towards me
And look up into my eyes.
Let your heart embrace the image you bear,
My image,
My hope,
My bright light.
You are fully accepted, always by my side.
These curvy edges, thin scars, and still-tender
bruises
Can't stop me from loving you,
Can't stop me from choosing to accept you,
Can't stop me from making you my very own,
My daughter,
My beloved. You are created as a portrait of my
infinite grace,
Every brushstroke purposefully painted,
All your finite failures covered by my presence.
Nothing you do, girl, can tear away this garment
draped round your shoulders.
Nothing you do can rip away this robe of
blameless purity.
Nothing you do can soil this shining white gift of
mine
That washes away your still-bloody scars with

gentle touch.
You are already pure as the bride you hope to be
In that longed-for wedding day dream that you
hold so close,
To be admired as complete in beauty and worth.
All this because you are loved,
Loved because I love,
Loved because I am love. Girl, you are precious to
me and filled with worth,
From golden green eyes to long tangly hair,
From aching hurt and regret to bursting joy and
comforting desire.
You are more valuable to me than any man's
affection,
Than any man's words,
Than any man's forceful touch.
You are accepted beyond rejection,
Beyond fear,
Beyond the past,
And are invited into my open arms, strong and
safe.
All this because I love you.
So turn away from your pain,
Away from your shame,
Away from the toil of proving yourself,
And set your eyes on me.
Set your eyes on the One who knows every part of
you
And loved you still, Who sets your soul free and
heals your heart,

Who wants you close by His side,
The author and perfecter of your faith,
Your heavenly father and only salvation, Your
life's breath and heart's satisfaction.
Now let yourself be loved, dear girl.
Won't you let me love you?

Mary Scarborough

Mary is a true friend, a calming presence, and a leader by example. She loves coffee, her family, and working with people. Mary offers whatever needs to be given and persistently sees the good in others. When reading and writing poetry, Mary quests after beauty, marveling at the vistas along the way. When she returns, she brings with her a fresh depiction of grace and redemption.

A Fool's House

Past the locked gate is my home,
through the grounds we shall roam.

At my roughhewn porch I ramble,
here I make my gamble.

By selfishness my rooms are filled,
with my wills that are billed.

My roof has many leaks,
because my mind is too weak.

Lord, help me fear thee
that I may a temple be.

VII

Look back on time with kindly eyes,
He doubtless did his best;
How softly sinks his trembling sun
In human nature's west!

Face the moon with a glowing heart
She boldly did her best;
How quick she raises her rippling tides
In seas from east to west!

3

Let me not to the marriage of true love.
I vow to never hear its golden ring,
Shall I cherish the silence of a dove,
And shy away from shining bells that sing?
O no, it chirps an ever-fixéd note
That can stir my heart 'lone from lone delight!
In you I hear this lovely chime I quote,
With you I hear this wand'ring sound I fight.
But now I listen to the bell's rhyme swell
And oh how the chyme can tell from my cell,
And oh how the molten-golden notes dwell,
Love cannot help but swing and ring the bell.
      And therefore never ask love not to be,
      For the bell will toll and it tolls for thee.

Composed in front of Elizabeth's Tower; 17 October 1857

I watched as closely as a tow'r
That stands on high o'ver steam and smoke,
And ticks and tocks upon each hour,
Till at once sleeping streets awoke;
Running to work, rushing to class,
Bumping and shoving as a mass.

Contin'ous as the River flows
And floods the next city and town,
They with the current go, yet do not know,
Where all the lost time again drowns:
The whole world saw I for a second
That's what time is worth, I reckon.

The fog beside them blurs; but they
Swim through their teemed company.
A pupil could not be but prey
To such a horde of gluttony:
I toll—and toll—yet no one hears
What thoughts and dreams they all endear.

Across the Thames, Above the Bridge,
I sit, led no more by the ring,
And fill the void of the imperfect pitch
With running, rushing, and bumping;
And then my heart's clock is too late,
And I'm the disheartening state.

Merry

Sparrow, Sparrow, oh so sarrow
How is your foor flight?
With bluezy drops y genis stops
And soley I fall dismerry.

Merry, Merry, quite conairy
How is your jarden jay?
Con bluezy trees and genis weeds
And cheppy Mates all mockinggay.

Ancient Ruins

Man's first feat is a fall,
His ample act to all.
His former god's a muse,
And art can only lose.
For truth and drama bind,
And ruins are left behind,
But beauty is still spoken,
So nothing is ever broken.

Gypsies

Here, a free flower for you!
But wait, it's never free--
Without a euro or two.
Oh roses and violets,

In their red and blue leaves,
Dancing still in my hands,
Until the Free, from countries rich
Their clothes, and cameras draw,

Why, I will give freely to them—
But wait, spare a cent!

He Calls My Name

What if I say I shall not go?
What if I am the start to a fall,
and leave, ashamed, from thee?
What if I break this world off,
See the gap between, — You and I, —
A wade in limbo?

I cannot go any further, —
Lust may sing, and desire may consume;
Undeserving now, to me,
As love fills my every hour,
And afar I hear my name,
And know I shall go!

Sarah Scott–Cruz

Sarah loves travel, rock climbing, milkshakes, and people (even when she thinks she doesn't). Driven and calm under pressure, she consciously strives to make the world a better place. Animals are her friends and she takes nothing for granted, even in literature. Sarah dives deep below the surface of a poem where she discovers unforeseen treasure.

Epigram

All things are foul fair: none can I see;
Things happen for reasons unknown to me.
Reality mocks prideful perception;
Real life oft falls short of self-deception.

Breaking the Horse

Fear is the filly on which my life rides,
Her unbroken back throws me side to side.
She needs to be groomed, to be touched and
tamed,
Because right now she's halting me from loving
your name.

You trace my back and say that it is strong,
But overlook the strength of the back that I ride
on.
You try to tame me, but the beast is within,
My fight is not yours, don't try to win.

The future is stable where my filly lives
Though stable it is not, she feeds on it
Taking off at a galloping gait
Dragging me away from you, my soul mate.

My filly kicked you again and again.
Until finally you limped back to Big Ben.
Galloping west as you flew east,
I knew I had chosen the beast.

You've tamed me enough so I don't flee,
But my fear still told me to set you free.
Waiting is no problem, your plea I refused.
All I got myself was trampled and bruised.

Mysterum Fidei

Hope but a blind and costly froth
Amongst the deep churning vat
Jostles and jumbles little skiffs
Whose angst'd draft obscures the Fish.

Far from current midst stormy seas
where shallowing waters lie
Whispers of want run skiffs aground
Doubts dew promise parched the mouth

Lost—torn canvas, progress unmade
Nets cast for fish—vain do prey
Thwart indifference—aimless wane
Nothing—better than what 'tis.

Unto Ends beyond
Trust the way
Eden—horizon
Faith—the ray.

Sonnet

When in pursuit that beast so patient reigns
My heart in—bitted by amoroso
So potent I swoon for you, humble Swain,
Awakening to an empty chateau
Deserted. I alone must muck out stalls
Of your delight and my surfeit of love
But still my senses were for you enthralled,
Thou amorist makes me a mourning dove.
This love is torment which causes squall—
I chomp at the bit, raring for free rein—
Lust is the love that leads my soul to fall
No longer, since I discern your true feign.
      My raining beast once pawed in all affairs
      But now dost flee with truer lines a'paired.

A World Without Butterflies

I met a wrinkled woman who survived
Stamped by flaxen star, scarlet 'pon her chest
Who said: Butterflies etched by hands pint-sized
Splattered red with vibrant dreams now hollow
Hopes—lead infused, unfathomable changed
Look at the butterflies, stuck on the wall—
Remember when they lived? the innocent
Broken and beaten to chambers they crawl
Hopeless and homeless, lost in the maze's cries!—
Acclimated to the stench of lives spent
Imagine a world without butterflies:
An unmoved unchanged eternal winter
That blackens the nak'd heart and bleeds the eyes
Hope not for a world without butterflies.

Instinct S

Italian pairs, larshing new
Voited tip, aggressive shoe
Divly tight, kurled orange and black
Scarpas[1] grindle my foot inflac:
    Toe begin, wiggle and whingle
    Gurring the loops with both middle fingers
    Knocked on my back, wroll blumbling with
the waves
    Clatching me tighter, life shhwoooouped
from my fingers
    With every movement, Scarpas grow
tighter.
    CRACK—a break from gurring—was it
ankle, wrist, or neck?
    Point through the top loop shining, not like
the blackeled two in back
    Up, and squeeesing-more heel out-to
darkling loops I bend
    Pull up, push in, wrest'd afoot Scarpian
friend
    Snackle, nuk, toekcappp, last pop—the
sound booms from within
    Phewee, owwie—one Scarpa underfoot.

Wrestling the Scarpas takes me back
The Rasta[2] years: red yell'w green and black
In Shaman[3] days when velcro sang
oh how my feet had so few pains!

49

But alas, the climb is hard
and Scarpas do clintch-cluntch the way.
My ninjian Scarpas grip the wall
and painfully too my happy feet.
In roomious evolvs I stabbishly swam.
But now can snappely say:
Nessun Luogo E' Lontand[4]

[1] Outdoor sports brand from Italy.
[2] Special edition of Shaman shoe.
[3] Shoe designed by Chris Sharma, pro-climber;
made by evolv.
[4] No Place too Far.

The Trevi Fountain

Trevi do you hear me?
    Though your scaffolds line the sky
    Imprisoned, barred, and bandaged
    Let not that dim your light.
Trevi are you sleeping?
    When will your waters move?
    Drowned by preservation
    I hope you will stir soon.
Trevi are you lonely?
    Kept still in Roman dark
    Remember lovers' kisses—
    Keep them close to heart
Trevi have you more to give?
    We wish upon your well
    Throw some coins back out at us
    If weight's too much to heal.
Trevi do you wish?
    Like travelers at your banks
    Returned to Rome, oh! what a dream
    Restored to lover's gaze.
Trevi do you miss it?
    The love and kisses and coins
    The hopeful footsteps from three roads
    Intersecting, brimming with life—
Trevi do you hear me?
    La Dolce Vita awaits
    Awaken please, spring water free
    We miss your grand beauty.

Parthenon's Pleas

Do you miss me? she asked
    Walls have been torn down
Did you kiss me? she asked
    Columns crumbling to the ground
Did you look at me when I stood strong?
    a roof above your head
Or now since left in ruins
    Do you notice what you had —
Did you dance with me? she asked
    Before I fell to Turks
Do you dance upon me now?
    with somber earnest bursts
Do you remember how I stood?
    just five short years ago
Was it different than today? she asked
    Or has time been preserved —
Did you love me in your innocence?
    Bobbed hair, bright eyes
Do you thank me now, experience?
    Take nostalgia…distant times:
For I stand here, a reminder,
    that broken is not dead.
If ruin befell your baby heart
    Since last our eyes did meet
Please leave your ruins at my feet
    and take a small piece of me:
Remember that change is all
    that is or e'er will be —

The sky went dark, cloud-covered sun,
　　And as the wind persisted
I could have sworn I heard her pleading
　　whisper,
　　　　　stay a while?

Athínai

Every city has its charm
but some are more enchanting.
London was a whirlwind
    Excitement was the feeling
    Adrenaline pumping, tickled tum—
    a first kiss kind of feeling.
Rome was a rolling sea
    longing was the feeling
    Though old surrounds, the city between
    Dampened the trickling breeze—
Athens was a sunny day
    Contentment was the feeling
    Ruins round walking embraced my heart
    Calmly I ran so freely.
Rome so close to Athens but yet, so far away
Rome flirts with fantastic
    Beckons whist and lust romantic
But Athens strings my heart along
    with golden thread of old
To return, I know not when,
but Athens shall be home.

Heartbeat

Stillness   in the moment—
         creates a stirring peace
Stillness for a moment
         demands a restless beat.
Hearts together, run apart—
Beat still my innocent child:
         Beating still becomes a man
                  Beat on against the current.

Take the World in Stride

Drive away the feeling of
Insecurity. Fortify the walls
with mean congruency. Keep
Still what is; let change never be
Apart

      grows the good and evil tree.

Above all questions answered
Above all things are one
Above no war or violence
Above no love at all—

So drive away the feeling of
control over all things. Fortify your walls
with vicissitude please. Keep
Still what is—changing seas.
Apart
      lives nothing but apathy.

Whispers Vast

Sit alone along the shore
Wish not for company
enough surrounds to fill the soul
be still and watch the sea.

As you sit, you are alone
Apart amongst the sea
The tide swells up and then recedes
be still it beckons thee.

As you watch, your eyes alone
Wander the coastal shore
As birds above span far and soar
but still you keep awhile.

Slowly shift your soft-eyed gaze
and sit in awe of sound—
The swiftly rushing hushing sea
sighs to touch your soul.

As you sit in silence
Listen soully to the sea
and realize dear there's much to see
apart from you and me.

Leisl Seigler

Leisl loves home, music, the violin, sweet tea, and her car Jeffrey. She is a natural caretaker. Her organization is a byword among her classmates, and is evident even in her poetry: she plants words into neat rows, where she tends them, until they offer life and beauty.

Expected Lies

A deafening roar, a rippling mane;

Cold blooded strength to ward off all pain.

His pride expects much, so he follows its will.

His coat glistens when seen from afar;

This satisfies his pride, so none look closer.

But this lion is lying inside,

Knowing full well all he does is hide.

Look closer, you'll see his matted coat and tangled
mane;

Scars shroud his seemingly flawless display.

Oh God, can this be me?

This lonely, lying lion here fails epically.

My heart screams in pain, though none can see;

All they want is a roar out of me.

So I roar my lonely lie to please the pride;

Yet, I have failed You.

Oh God, have mercy on me.

Sonnet 1

The sonorous flutes so sweet, so soft;
Violins trill wonderful words of love
That ebb and swell with passion borne aloft;
Your music, players, coos as a dove.
But clash! Cymbals crash-
Trumpets flare- drums roll-
Violins scream- flutes gnash-
Dear God, oh please release this soul!
At last, the music calms and again
Does sing so sweetly its song of love.
Beauty in chaos, beauty in pain-
So lovely and gentle as the dove.
And thus is my love for you, Xander*;
Never dying, ever in flux, in grandeur.

Violin of the author.

Blood and Tears

The sun shone bright
Through the stormy blight.
As its blood pumped fierce,
Through the earth the tiny seedling pierced.

The earth became hot as fire
And it was drained of blood.
The little plant was dry
And couldn't even cry.

The earth was cooler
And the blood red leaves became its cover.
The flowers bent and died,
And now the plant cried.

The air is frigid.
The stem of your love is rigid.
The pain of its death
Makes you cry blood and tears.

To Ms. Jensen
Written by a student, eternally grateful for all that
you've done.

The Blonde Little Lady

A student there was with an air of frustration
At certain genres of literature, they say.
Said student would groan and lament every time
She had to read poetry, and even to write.

This distaste was known by everyone 'round:
Not even a secret to biology teachers.
Til long came a quiet small blonde little lady
Who'd quickly turn 'bout this student's
frustration.

"Just try it," said that blonde little lady
And slowly, but surely, her (stubborn) student
responded.
At first it was simply a labor for grades;
Then somewhat enjoyable, not just for a grade.

And suddenly from inside this writer there came
An unexplained love for the thing she once hated.
"See, you can do it," the blonde lady told her;
Quite honestly the first time she'd ever been told.

And from that one compliment, it started a love

Not just for the subject, but for the blonde lady,
too.
She seemed to accept and support the student's
writing
And constant life updates and life's good ole
dramas.

And so the blonde lady became like a sister
To her new student who shared in her passion.
Ms. Jensen, I thank you for all that you've done.
You've changed me forever. I'll never forget you.

I Sat Down to Write

My soul desired to speak,
So I sat down to write.
I'm not sure what it needs to peep,
But I know this feels right.
It seems to be happy,
From what I can tell.
I just Skyped my baby-
Perhaps that's why it swells.
Or maybe, perchance, it beams
From saving a place at home just for me.
Whatever it is, I know one thing's sure-
Poetry had never come so nat'rally to me.

Man of God

Do you hear the bells?
Yes, they ring afar,
But often fear does swell
And, truly, I'm at war.

Will the man I know and love
Become the man I need for life?
Does he know he needs to shove
His boyishness off to the side?

He holds my hand with seeming strength,
But inside he is weak.
When will he understand
That he a stronger hand must seek?

Never forget, my man of God,
From where your strength doth flow;
And know that when you seek Him first,
I'll fall in step behind,
And sink into the strength of you,
My strongest earthly leader.

I'll love you deeper than the ocean blue,
And you will deeper love me, too.
And if your Maker be before you,
Who could be against you?
Be my man of God, sweet love, and we'll turn out
just fine.

My Heart Sings for You

Rolling green fields of grass like an ocean,
Hidden flow'r gardens buzzing with life;
The beauties they hold give me the notion,
That something about you is paradise.

Tall bricked buildings, trimmed in white,
Housing the people of this generation.
Each of them brings me delight.
There needs to be more like you in this nation.

Truly, I love you and can't wait to see you.
The first time I met you, my heart ached with joy.
When you wrapped your arms 'round me, I knew
that you'd do.
Samford, my darling, my heart sings for you.

My Shrobant Jeffrey

'Twas a shirning day; a day so shirning
One failed to see the froaming fhere up in the sky.
A shroyous breeze flished among the cars,
Among those my fanshnazzy Jeffrey.

His shribiant white shleamed from his sholsterous
steel.
His trunk, snoasting a sporty tailfin, opened with
a
Shlick and shnop, and in my heart something
grew.
His shood, oh his shood! Oh how I love him so!

Shappy the day I drove off with him!
Shappy the day I smushed the pedal and
Shoom! Away we zwang!

The Knife

Oh you wicked Knife!
Oh you deceitful Wretch!
Oh how you tease, toss, and tear
The soul.

You! You knew you would hurt.
You knew you would lie and only
Allow glimpses of forever.
You Demon!

Here, a day or two.
Here, a week or so.
Why? Why do you torture me so?

Hypocrite!
Don't tell me it's easy!
Don't lie to my face!
You- you- Distance!

To Rome

I saw your grandeur from afar
And my mind flew to your glorious peaks.
I sat upon your broken ramparts,
Gazing at your ruined seats.
Think of the thousands who stood below—
Viewed your blood soaked floors—
Strained their voices at the show—
To think!
The gladiators who sweated and shook,
Waiting to be raised to your genius arena—
The animals, starved and angry,
Preparing to tear apart any in their paths—
To think!
But to see—
I saw your majesty, your ingenuity.
I beheld your magnificent arches, your sparkling
eyes.
To think— to see—
Contradiction in all your splendor,
I love you even as you fall.

Watch Me

Tell me-
How do you think it is?
Tell me-
What is it like to hate life?
Tell me-
Do you even know?
    No answer?
  Surprise, surprise.

Black mail- your last resort.
How sad- you're never even there.
All me- no one can help.
But I can't win?
      Oh.
     Watch me.

Watch me trample darkness with light.
Watch me love, deeper than the ocean, myself and
life.
Watch me climb this mountain and roar from its
summit
"I have won. I am done.
     You
    Were wrong".

Catherine Uritis

Catherine once sheared a Scottish sheep. She is spontaneous, has terrible timing, and enjoys Latin puns. She longs to see, know, and study as much as she can. She plans to continue her studies of art, classics, and the humanities. Catherine intertwines herself and her words with a poem until it's part of her and it bursts forth into a lush, vivid blossom.

Epigram I

Relieved to know that Hearts still yearn
Without ours there to break, —
For passing we are passers on
Of many Joys of fate.

A Response to The Hollow Men

We are the broken men
we are the shattered men
how our roar shakes as we
stand together

Screams revolve in dreams
In Satan's black kingdom
there is banished to there
here, the day perches on
the edge of a strong column
here, the lark is singing
and songs are
no longer fleeting
more real and more prism
than a gossamer snow

The suffering was there
there was suffering there
In that gulley of shattered mirrors
that gutter of shards
that last goodbye of man's last kingdom

let me cast the cloak
in God's new kingdom
let me shed the wear
all the rest
wet coat, torn skin, glass eyes,
in the fields

becoming what was meant
nothing less

lightless until
lights appeared
as the saving hope
the multifold rose
of our final kingdom
the nameless Something
of broken men

This is the living land
this is the milk land
here the honey trickling
is scooped with, clutched
with the fingers of relieved men
under the glow of a beating sun

broken not hollow
bent not empty

for now is
and time is
and thine is
our kingdom

So this is the way the world begins
not with a hope but a dance

Sonnet 1

Did you happen to prick your finger, love?
Before you painted your feelings away
Did you mix yourself into the hues, love?
When you stuck soul to paint to board that day
Oh did you scrape a scrap of skin, my dear,
When coursing ink ran through blue veins?
Oh did your words charge through the page, my
dear,
Like bulls in these little blue lanes?
When tempests turn and twist and toil and try,
Ne'er fear! For you are with the truest lot!
When worlds implode and with the dogs you lie,
Look up to stars! See what marv'lous stories
they've got.
      If souls be twisting tendrils usually held in
keep,
      Ah my friend, the artist's body must have
sprung a leak.

(Ode To Byron)

When a knave has no shelter nor solace in hand,
Let him share his troubles and woes.
Let him open his heart to the rest of his band,
And soon find himself amongst foes.

The importance of friends is a curious thing,
Which has nev'r been truly tested.
So admit your struggles to all those listening,
And if not deserted, detested.

Kiu Parolas Esperanton?

You'd think- it lived!
You'd say: it spoke,
Their Days-gone by- their bugle blows
The Words-they danced
The men-they said
Were brought up from dead
When they read that printed Page

Oh the ages- roll by
Our portraits- they fade
Our legacy- but let this- remain

We- who undid the
Great Done of God,
We who Knitted our own-
No more will Babble crack its whip-
We enlightened are better off alone

When the Tower was first cast down,
And the shattered columns remained
The Wasteland- it ruled
The dogs- they spoke
More crystalline than their human folk
Like rats on dust,
They prattled, they pawed-
We the Cast Down Sons of God

But! now! You see!
Time is but a tool-
With which- we fix
The err'rs of elder fools:

We have mastered the Word-
We have been gods
Language bends and twines for us
The master at last
-Conquered the past-
Recalled the future
On this great surface clock we live
We live- and Talk- and Tock
For if you ask on this new dawn-
"Kiu parolas Esperanton?"
Or: "Who speaks Esperanto"
Our legacy-be that-
The answer be: all!
Resounding from below

"Made Cunningly"

A world lives in my shadow-
as if a galaxy were pinned down
by the tips of my toes
the little planets buzzing low
like a bee in a circle goes
always round and round
-cyclical bound-

A forest rides on my voice-
like i had swallowed
all the birds and they sing
-not by my choice-
like bells- their voices ring
preventing sadness to wallow
and words from seeming hallow

A wind is bottled up inside my eyes
as if I were a storm ready to break
always ready to roam far
and yearning to cast off ties
maybe to some celestial star
at the end of the dead earths wake
-If only this dream I could shake-

The Flight of Zebdegah

Zebdegah rilled down that tibly path
And jumping and jalumping did that fairy laugh
All mimsili and bubsily skipping
And tripping, Zebdegah always tripping

She skippered through the libush greenish dew
To the sound of the trilling and lulling of the
Modaboo
Flushing and falling she flew through the air
Towards that smithuous town called Dobbledare

And in that lippel town there squat a man
And his zebby wife and the zest of his clan

This man called Brushelpop was the pop of a thing
The most thingiest thing of all sorts of things
This thing was a boy with a fatumous gold curl
That shung on his top with a plumponing twirl

While the tot totter-teetted and his curl bibbled
about
That Zebdegah slied the thing from her barmey
route
Swooshing she pounced like the renown
BeddleBouse
And she swished-swashed him right up into her
pouch

All Dobbledare yawped and shot at the air
Hoping to trop the nixious fairy right there
But Zebdegah crockled and snipped far away
Saving the boy in pouch for another day

Her slinkering lips slithered a smile
She escaped through the mash and all its green
bile

Zebdegah snapped back to her path
And jumping and jalumping did that fairy laugh
All mimsili and bubsily skipping
And tripping, Zebdegah always tripping

Written After Getting Lost in Ostia Antica

We play on the bones of an old city-
The bricks decaying at last-
We run though the cracks and the corners-
And prick our bare feet on the grass.

The pines hang up like plumes
Of some exotic bird long gone-
Who maybe used to live in this city-
Before the rough times as always led on.

We trace the stones of the ancients-
And feel the balmy spring air-
Knowing that someone else once stood
And felt the same thing in that very there.

And I know that one day I'll be in an old city-
That in my youth was new-
And that someone will come exploring-
Just as these friends and I used to do.

And then who will I be but the Romans?
Another old face gone in time gone by-
But the difference I find with the Romans
Is they left things far after they died.

Things used to be built to last-
And now just maybe renewed-

So maybe my city will never be
By far future eyes even viewed.

Olympian

We are Zeus and Athena
Hera, Demeter, and more
We are immortal and
immoral and the stuff of lore

We are the rulers of oceans
and skies and vast lands
We sip honey and nectar
reclining in our merry bands

The world goes mad
every day, every year
We could try to fix it
but it's more pleasant from up here

And what if we try?
and- fear to say- fail
Best let it stand
and lift not the painted veil

We are Poseidon and Hades
Or Hermes or Artemis who enthralls
But perhaps we are mortals
just playing on pedestals

Kingdom Come

The Queen on her gossamer throne with skill,
And a pale moon face, and a rosen smile,
Awakening soft souls on dawn unTill
Away, she must away from this sweet isle.

So the Joker of good faith and sword
Takes up good Councell for the daring fight,
And strives and sings joyfully unto the Lord
Of cheer and hope he is God's good knight.

As the Heir ascends on the brightest hour,
The purple parade flies to dusk it's close.
A hope from Jentle yellow of her flower
Now in the honey land peace overflows.

Four years have gone and only one remains,
Though all have shared and molded these our
brains.

Benjamin Yates

Ben likes books, empty places, and dead things--
mostly people and languages. He enjoys the smell
of typewriters at 12 AM, the smell of tea at 2 AM,
and the smell of bed at 4 AM. In his spare time, he
edits books for his classmates. He wants to study
classics and reveres the sonnet. Ben unearths the
essence of poems, carefully re-piecing fragmented
ideas and images into the whole, beautiful form
that was always intended.

The Elegy of Mr. J. Alfred Prufrock

"Nonetheless, our men could not keep ranks or
get a firm foothold, neither were they able to
follow the standards; rather, different men from
different ships grouped round whatever standard
they ran up against, and they were in great
confusion."
Caesar, *Gallic Wars*

The ideal woman, you ask?
She is short, fat, buxom, and weak,
With rolls of fat surrounding her buttcheeks —
And an ever–present desire to eat.

....

I'm sorry I have offended you. To jest
Often is what I crave, though every moment
Carries his new sorrows,
I must exhume the grave, dust off the corpse,
and
Bring him into tomorrow.

But the yellow–and–green body rots
With the stench of time; all my
Last–weekends end up buried beneath his
eyeballs—
Which reminds me, I never paid the tab at that
Bar with the strange lot out back,
A very surly pack

Of fellows who wish to draw you in and ask,
"How many years since
    You have lived?

                Ten?"

I only feel alive
When reading diatribes.

The mountains that rise and sink
Beneath the touch of a thousand cares,
The trees that yield to the snares
Of a thousand certainties, cutting like an axe
To fell all your fears and hopes.
What remains, but the times
And times and times to be tied down
With the absurdities of the moment, the ropes
That bind you to that chair, to listen to me
Prate on and on about uncertainty.

I end, I cease, I have no more to say.
The moment dries up, decays,
Leaving me dehydrated of meaning
Lost in the caves of last month's newspapers —
I have forgotten to live, to pick up my dry
cleaning.

Swiftly Moving Tide

Lord, how can I reach that fateful ground?
I am but a swiftly moving
tide:
Yet from the sea I have found
A vision of that blessed place
The strength of which, I have not to face.

Holy Fire that dost burn the souls of men
Vaporize my meager substance now
With the heat of thy mind;
Among the heavens I shall dwell:
Free from this wretched form, the accursed
swell.

Trials and attempts, surges and efforts,
acquiesce;
But combined and fused, wrought
No progress. Yet eternal bliss
Hath rained me upon that gracious land,
Eternal's grace bestowed, forevermore to stand.

You are Ben

You are disabled. You are Ben Yates, too, but first, you are disabled. You are disabled and you are Ben Yates and you have cerebral palsy and he does not like you. He has never liked you and your blonde hair and your withered hand and funny limp and excuses from gym class. You are disabled and you see him coming towards you with that sneer on his face. You are disabled and you are scared, scared for the fiftieth, no, sixtieth time that day, for you are weak. You are disabled and you are Ben Yates and his fist hits your crotch like a brick wall. You are disabled and you are Ben Yates and for that moment, for that fraction of a second, you know you exist. But you would rather not exist as the pain radiates up your body and fills your eyes with tears.

You are disabled and you are Ben Yates and thank you very much, but I can't come to the pool party. You are Ben Yates and you never go to pool parties. You are disabled and you are Ben Yates and the only thing you can swim in is your own tears at night, when you crawl into bed and beg God to fix you, to make you whole and give you fists to fight and legs to swim and muscles to flex. You are disabled and you would rather not be.

You are disabled and you are Ben Yates and this hospital gown is much too revealing. You are disabled and you are Ben Yates and you cannot urinate, the doctor informs you, because the anesthesia from the surgery has had an adverse reaction with your body. You are disabled and the nurse explains what a catheter is, and how she will need to ram it down a tube you prefer no one to ram things down. You are disabled and you are Ben Yates and you are ashamed, ashamed of your weakness, ashamed of this nurse pressing a plastic tube down your orifice, and ashamed of your wretched legs that won't allow you to walk out of this damn hospital and this damn life you never asked for.

You are disabled and you are Ben Yates and the pool is cold. The pool is cold but your friend's smile is warm and you hope the warmth from his smile will warm the pool up, so you get in. You are Ben Yates and you have briefly forgotten you are disabled as you wade slowly to the deepest depth you can go without drowning. You are Ben Yates and you remember you are disabled when you suddenly drop below the water and your nose fills with chlorine and your friend grabs your arm and pulls you up.

You are disabled and you are Ben Yates but you decide that you will swim. You are disabled but you push off the wall of the pool and beat the water with your good hand and good leg and hope you will make it halfway. You are disabled but you have been trying to make it halfway for a month now. You are disabled but you make it half way and you draw your head out of the water and yell triumphantly. You are disabled and you are Ben Yates and the entire pool looks at you, but you don't care. You made it halfway.

You are Ben Yates and you have finished your 25th lap. You are Ben Yates and you lift yourself out of the pool. You are Ben Yates and the lifeguard eyes the scars on your legs but you don't care, you finished your 25th lap. You are Ben Yates and others can swim better than you, but you don't care, for you are Ben Yates, you are disabled, and you know what it means to fight and win.

Love Unlimited

The following poem is an imitation of Chaucer's Canterbury Tales, *in which various pilgrims tell their stories on a pilgrimage to Canterbury. The following tale is told by the Friar, who, contrary to his monkish office, is secretly licentious.*

The tale I do venture to let escape
These sinful lips and tongue most vile and black
Is one of contrary structure and shape –
For it flows from not this besotted mind
But from a Love divine, free from sin's attack.

O night more blessed than the bright and hot
Day – bring to us with thy cool embrace
Unknown virtues of sweet pleasure; and plot
The course of a poor fellow's sultry talk.
Be silent now, fellow pilgrims, in God's good
grace.

There once was a fair wench known as Penelope
Whose beauty shined brightly in her homeland
Of Ithaka; her eyes were blue and free
Of fraud and greed and all evil desires –
She was more beautiful than most could stand.

But this blessed woman was bound to a
most worthless, contemptible wretch, a fraud:

Ulysses, man of many ways and many hates.
He hated God, our Savior, and the Blessed Virgin
Most of all. He was more than completely flawed.

It came to pass that Ulysses was called
away to Ilium. For there, deceit and lies
were in most high demand. His bald
misdeeds found full support in pagan Greeks.
And every wicked man mourned his "God-be-
byes."[1]

Midway along the journey of her life
Penelope awoke to find herself
Amidst a dark and wooded state of fog:
Cut from that cord that gave her life and love
She had no hope, no life, no faith, no health.

So when the lusty, good men of fair Ithaka
Had seen the sordid state of such a fair
And comely wench, and since they heard of all
mythical
Cruelty on the part of shameful Ulysses,
Then they decided that something must pierce her
despair.

Antinoös, the most giving among
These saints, spoke unto all: "Friends, lovers,
Ithakians, lend me your ears; and unsung

---

[1] A medieval phrase meaning "goodbye." Derived from "God be by you."

Harmonies of our sweet and buxom queen
Behold. For between the blue and white bedcovers

Of our most precious Madonna there chimes
The bells of a vacancy. For what well-equipped
woman
Doth wish to stay unbedded for so long a time?
Come then, sweet brothers, and bring your hands
and instruments
And partake of this queen's sweet goods.

And speaking thus, he led the suitors to
The queen's most sumptuous halls, and there
They ate and drank most fully of her rich beef
stew.
And after the meal the queen descended from
chambers
On high and invited every man to enjoy a more
prized brew.

And she engendered there, every day, with a
different saintly suitor,
And in time, she begot many children, by many
fathers, with many blessings from on high, and all
the children were healthy and full of the love of
God. And all dwelt in peace in the redeemed
household of Penelope, and love was free and full
of the Holy Spirit.

And when the news of Ulysses' gruesome death at
Ilium

Reached the throbbing halls, Penelope lifted her
hands in praise,
And thanking Him from whom all lovers flow, she
said, "Thy will be done, on earth,
As it is in heaven. Shantih, shantih, shantih.[2]"

[2] T.S. Eliot says this Sanskrit word is best translated
"the peace which passeth all understanding."

To Ida

"We mounted upward through the rifted rock,
And on each side the border pressed upon us,
And feet and hands the ground beneath required."
-Dante, *Purgatorio*

When Dawn with her rosy fingers
Comes prowling 'cross the star-set sky –
I think of you, my love, and of
That bloodied pleasure-filled climb
Up the craggy rocks of Mount Ida.

These rocks we crossed with our romantic feet
Did with rage and love once meet.
Yet time, that ever-nagging wench, still found
them incomplete.
So parting at once and ever, they swelled in
lasting heat.
But our steps did these fickle fissures cross,

And when some poor unfated Trojan shot the
Albatross
With brazen bow and spirit,
We did but inherit his grief
Atop Mount Ida.

So now the day drags on
And with a spirit forlorn
I stare at the blue-black angel
That guards your grave.
And if I were to follow her stony gaze,
She would be looking westward,
To Ida.

Sweet Darling Love

O lead me to that path of pathways
Where life and love and food begin anew—
Sweet darling of my airport fever–stay,
Oh please, my love, come to my timely rescue.
Your comely paper form is near my view,
But oh! Your thick plastic scent is smelt
By another man's nose. But as I rued
The day I stepped into your home, I felt
A small but sure tapping upon my pelt:
"Good sir," quoth he, in thick Wisconsin, "you
Seem to have dropped your boarding pass." Dealt
A blow, but one of joy! And spoke he true
For in his hands was my sweet darling love,
Sent straight to me from powers above.

She is Beauty

She is beauty.

She is beauty when you see her from a block away,
jumping rope,
When you walk by and say hello,
And she acknowledges your presence, in all its
awkwardness,
She is beauty.

She is beauty in the yellow mornings when your
thoughts are late assignments
And your breath is stress, metallic and tart,
When a thick fog envelops you, and your sight
leaves you,
She is beauty.

She is beauty when nothing else is, when the
world creaks on its hinges
And Atlas resigns his duties as watchman of the
madness,
When suffering is dominant and the Future is
dead, lying in his casket,
She is beauty.

She is beauty in your prosperity,
In the golden moments of collegiate glory beheld
by all,

When laughter flows like mead thick and rich, and
you are certain of certainties,
She is beauty.

She is beauty in the middle times,
In the times after glory and struggle, when that fat
slug, Time, slides on his belly
Ever-slow and secret, throughout your days,
covering you with slime,
She is beauty.

She is beauty when grey, the color of completion,
has tinted
Every last hair, and you sit rocking on your porch,
modest and small,
With her next to you, sweet in all her years,
bearing the fruit of experience,
She is beauty.

Natalia Yépez-Frias

Natalia speaks only when she has something to say. She loves Michael Buble, Peter Pan, and Hamlet. Simultaneously intense and playful, brilliant and absent-minded, serious and light-hearted, Natalia wants to apply her understanding of two different cultures to help others. Natalia first plunges headlong into a poem, and then dances through it with every fiber of her being intent. No detail is left unattended, no loveliness un-admired.

Epigram

Habits chiseled bear artful demeanors,
Just another in a world of mirrors:
A reflection that both blinds and defines,
Morphing not just perception but our minds.

The Masterpiece

Alone I stand, a crude canvas left untouched,
Undecided my artist paces,
The paints left intact,
The canvas is wanting, insecure of its identity,
Indecision soon spoils the man, abandoning thus
the canvas.
Another artist comes along and uses sinful
medium.
Satisfied with splatter of pride,
The artist leaves, the canvas left suffering,
Hearing the amorphous cry, artists arrive, filing in,
desiring but a turn,
All staining their screaming marks of influence.
The canvas lies accordingly unrecognizable,
Alone I stand, a canvas embellished with tiers o
triviality,
Illustrations of insincerity,
Imbrications of injustice, Beams of belligerence,
My artist returns, but really my artist no more.
This original man stares at the crucified canvas,
And frets of imperfections no more.
The erasure of the artist restored the previous,
The canvas stands alone no more,
With brush in hand and Will at heart He, the artist,
pencils,
Do I then shape myself?
Let me be a pochoir of Thy stencil,

Only when my identity lies in you will I be
painted true.
A feeble man no more this canvas stands.

Mine

The second stanza of the following poem by Emily Dickinson is an addition by the author.

Mine - by the Right of the White Election!
Mine - by the Royal Seal!
Mine - by the sign in the Scarlet prison -
Bars - cannot conceal!

Mine - one - Father - Founding Promise!
Mine - by the House Affirm!
Billed - the Ballot - Sake forlorn--
Mine - intern Right adjourn!

Mine - here - in Vision - and in Veto!
Mine - by the Grave's Repeal -
Titled - Confirmed -
Delirious Charter!
Mine - long as Ages steal!

Wet Eyed Smiles

Begotten child of mine reaps sweet bone break!
Meat grinding for scholarly succession!
Hark torture conceived for betterment's sake,
Yet yearly toll dry Peter's 'munition--
Incomplete lines of stressing ten feet!
In age, doubt: in birth, pain of loin of lamb.
Neverland, dreaded dream, loss 'Till defeat;
I am my only child, child that I am.
Brigade of beards and suits, hapless soul keep,
Mem'ry to Peter too shall surrender--
Weep for me, Peter, *both* too old to leap!
Unity in tears for clever crower!
Whence, communion of souls, child and mother,
"We few, we happy few, we band of brothers."

To the Lost Children

I   In silence I began.
       Hail to thee, blithe Mem'ry –
     Solace to wrongs of man!
       We, the cure for tragedy,
     Born to donate our investment vitality.

     A life not my own:
       A figure caught in mirror,
     A sculpture of stone,
       A wrinkle in the shimmer,
     Our cause declared to be for a world
greater.

     School a distraction
       Unifying pre-condemned souls.
     How could men sanction
       Hopeless youths paying tolls
     For the automated — supposed human –
fools?

II   In our world we find
       Beauty in each other:
     To forget, to remind
       Us: Children of the Gutter,
     Of innocent opportunity to be sister, mother

    –

For me I found my hope:
    His face a meadow
Seeding strength to cope
    With threat of garden fallow
From the hungry mortals, casting shadow.

III   Yet my solvent nature
    Turns myself against me.
How can there be such rapture?
    How do I breathe and be?
To live on borrowed time, still to yearn to
be free.

Like a shadowy specter
    Banished to Inexistence,
Leading life of conjecture,
    Hidden from sight, not as treasure, but
as treachery:

Like a paradoxical poem
    Artfully deceitful in meaning,
Bound to be lonesome
    When discarded, forever labeled:
Fleeting,

Like a convicted innocent
    Judged unjustly by the absolute court:
Guilty, Undesirable rodent,
    So simply, so quietly condemned to
mort–

Like a warm whisper
    Carrying secrets to the dark,
    Growing ever-fainter
       As the black-hearted drown and
strangle it for lark.

Cut short our lives are,
    Or as they say, complete.
    A tolerated blemish, scar
      Here we are to donate –
They cheat life, and we surrender to Death's
defeat.

IV   I saw my hope disabled,
      His heat of breath fogs no more
    Against the surgical table;
      Something missing from before,
I feel where it once pulsed, my heart, my
core!

Ask not if we have souls,
    Call me inhuman,
As thunder surely rolls,
    Should I echo the forgotten?
I am fated to caress this oblivion!

He was my life in this lifeless existence!

    As I feel embrace of wind, smiling of
sunrise,

Howling of grass, grainy kiss of salted
sand,
I imagine all my memories washed
ashore:

I imagine a twink'ling apparition
Growing on the vista with every nearing
step:
I imagine the waving of his hand and
The blurred shout of his greeting doth
soar —

I do not let myself imagine anymore.

V   All is left, but to wonder
At this life cut short.
No response to blunder,
Deaf-eared retort,
To good company in Death I resort.

I wonder if perhaps
The people whom we cure,
The people who set such traps,
Denying souls to assure,
Lead the same lives we endure.

Do we not all want more time?
Do we not all complete?
Listen to fading of feat,
To the unchanged chime –
In silence I will end ——

Phantoms and Stairwells

Saying what needs to be said is hard to say,
Soundingly, with all things having been said:
Un-used to unbreath, 'til final relinquay –
 O, Phantoms shoust I take me there instead?

Phantoms precede me vasternear
As snufferings or blunderghasts,
Shadows that from larkhigh aim to shnear
Princes and mermaids and bippity-boppidy boos!

Phantoms secress to soultheft.
Deceitful unbreath life – long for that of death!
Peace only when all known bereft
With the deepest longest relief of breath.

The Phantoms, guardians of losts,
Thumes of sprimps in vestibules and halls,
In dreams and stairwells and mosts,
In torious expelled, in exhaled ripcalls.

Phantoms it took to show ides!
Remind me of thy purgatorio,
Follow me into the airin deservides,
Exhume me into the swarrowing of times.

Heightasy falls far below, tis better to benear
beflow,
To know: chiggles and hickles no sign of health,

So phew in hearts and dreams, to live in stairwells.
It's not so yeeks here, to be as I, Phantom.
Never have I breathed so well as I did my last
breath.

Pietas

A moment — duty and hero —
Chattering footsteps chime cheer,
Shuffling coils chuckle in show,
Costing-words to souls do peer.

A moment — soak sincerity —
Possible to capture love of mother?
God, let us pray for kissed-clar'ty,
May spectacle silence all other.

Behold! Behold my Son.
At long last I see He is still.
My Sparrow, mina that has begun
The fulfillment of charged-bill.

Admire his slight frame,
Take in his gentle crumble,
Understand weighed-mean blame,
Humble the Icarus-rumble.
O, emptied-tongues, need I say, Son?
Brace me for your sweet disquiet,
Which mothers do so tear upon,
Affirming with oak-arms thank-Blight.

Be-sought for what is not –
Glory-rest His peaceful face,
Grace for the un-bought wrought –

Here, these stolid stand, even here, a here-and-
after case!

Let this be my silent lullaby
To You who redeem all with one fall.
I cry for fresh-blood, an ease-cry
For relieved-mercy in dying-sigh-call.

Let us once-before espouse gain with loss,
 Be mother, be father, I pass to un-last rest,
Take care of my human-God
Whose smooth-meek is filled-unfilled albatross.
Let be movements in marble as un-word would.
Sometimes silence is best.
Carry Cross.

Torture

Torture me 'til dead,

Torture me to tomb,

Team me with dried dread

That rises in One womb–

Threat'ning summer slumber;

Tame crusted coffin bloom,

Thank lonely sunder

To tender quaint consume.

Torture me to wakeful dreams,

Thrashing for spirited un-deeds.

It is the greatest freedom

To be more than meal to worm kingdom!

Mary Scarborough

In this puzzle world,
Though we are bent, cut, and gnarled,
Amongst these tones of bright and blue,
I thank the God above me for the chance to fit
alongside you.

As you drink your coffee –
Thinking of whom this speaks –
Recognize yourself in the freedom you let be,
In the angel-joy that flows to and from your
chipmunk cheeks,
In the first moments when fellows become friends;
Nowhere is there a Mary that to a garden better
tends.

Watch! You whistle wit and all do so turn to listen!
There are souls so pure, peaceful, and powerful,
That no matter the easy-smile, are profound and
wonderful.
Never underestimate the task for which you're
chosen.

Look upon the Cross which is of all good things
the source,
Be glad of what's behind you for it led you to this
course.
When I think of how a new start begins its dawn
And how every Now is gone, gone,

I never fear for what has been the best whirlwind
trip,
Since that is certainly the way for any timeless
friendship.

I don't yet know quite how we mix,
Conquering the world, or Tweedledee and
Tweedledum?
We have time! – Even when faded and wrinkled,
just think of the fun!
...Yet, as long as we're living I'll always be glad
for the most reliable of bricks,
The top of my picks, the gift of April two-en-ty-
and-six.

In this puzzle world,
Though we are bent, cut, and gnarled,
Amongst these tones of bright and blue,
I thank the God above me for the chance to fit
alongside you.

www.ingramcontent.com/pod-product-compliance
Lightning Source LLC
LaVergne TN
LVHW022317080426
835509LV00036B/2580